DISCARD

PARTNERS AND PARENTS

BY MICHAEL CHINERY

CHERRYTREE BOOKS

A Cherrytree Book

Designed and produced by
A S Publishing

First published 2000
by Cherrytree Press
327 High Street
Slough
Berkshire
SL1 1TX

British Library Cataloguing in Publication Data

Chinery, Michael
Partners and parents. — (Secrets of the rainforest)
1. Rain forest animals — Juvenile literature
2. Animal partners — Juvenile literature
3. Parents (Biology) — Juvenile literature
I.Title
591.7'34

ISBN 1 842 34000 X

Design: Richard Rowan
Artwork: Malcolm Porter
Consultant: Sue Fogden

Printed in Hong Kong by Wing King Tong Co. Ltd

Acknowledgements
Photographs: *All by courtesy of Michael & Patricia Fogden*
with the following exceptions: BBC Natural History Unit
9 centre, 10, 26, 28, 29; Michael Chinery
14 bottom, 15 bottom

❋ CONTENTS ❋

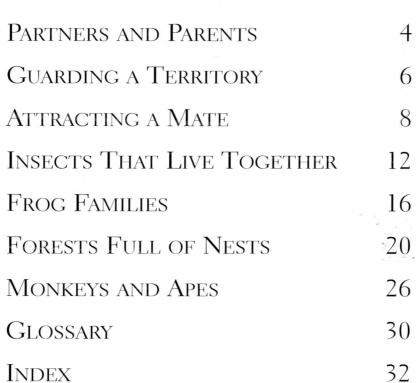

❂ PARTNERS AND PARENTS ❂

RAINFORESTS grow in the tropical regions around the equator, where temperatures are high all year and where it rains nearly every day. Trees and other plants grow thick and fast in these conditions. Animals also find the warm climate to their liking and huge numbers make their homes, find mates and bring up their young in the rainforests. But there is danger in the rainforest as well: lots of predators ready to catch and eat other creatures, especially youngsters.

   With so many enemies around, looking after babies is vitally important. Many rainforest animals are protected by camouflage or by being poisonous. Many others have well-developed social behaviour that ensures that their young are protected.

FENDING FOR THEMSELVES

Not all animals are good parents. Insects and many other small creatures do not look after their young at all. Butterflies and moths, for example, lay many eggs. They lay them on leaves that will nourish the caterpillars hatching from them, and leave them to the mercy of their enemies. Most of the caterpillars will be eaten by predators but there are generally so many that some are bound to survive into adulthood. Most frogs also lay large numbers of eggs and then abandon them. The majority of these eggs or the tadpoles that hatch from them are eaten by predators, and few survive to become adults.

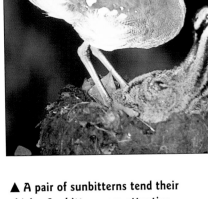

▲ A pair of sunbitterns tend their chicks. Sunbitterns are attentive parents, bringing food to their nestlings and scaring away intruders.

▼ A family group of tarsiers. Mammals mostly make good parents, feeding and caring for their young until they can fend for themselves.

METAMORPHOSIS

MANY insects and other small animals take no interest in their offspring. They never see how they grow up, nor witness the remarkable changes that some undergo. When a butterfly lays an egg, it hatches into a larva called a caterpillar. This has little stumpy legs and no wings. It eats and eats and eats, shedding its skin from time to time as it grows. After a while it undergoes another change and becomes a pupa. As a pupa it neither moves nor feeds, but its body slowly changes into that of an adult. The passionvine butterfly (left) has just emerged from its pupa, ready to begin its adult life. These changes are called metamorphosis, which means 'changing shape'. Frogs also metamorphose from eggs, to tadpoles, to frogs.

GOOD PARENTS

Animals, including birds and mammals, that look after their eggs and young give them a much better chance of survival, and they do not need to lay so many eggs or have many babies. After mating, males mostly go off and leave the females to rear the babies on their own, but some males make good fathers. Male birds often catch most of the food for their families. Mammals are particularly good parents, often living in family groups. Baby mammals have to stay with their mother for a time because they feed on their mother's milk.

▲ Most frogs lay lots of eggs, leave them and never see their offspring. The glass frog from the South American rainforest is different. The male and the female both guard their precious eggs.

▶ A mother eyelash viper and her brood. The newborn snakes are green or gold. Most snakes lay eggs but nearly all vipers give birth to live young.

GUARDING A TERRITORY

SOME ANIMALS have no homes. They wander through the forest, alone or in groups, eating wherever they find food and sleeping wherever they happen to be when they are tired. Most animals, however, have some kind of territory, which they defend against other animals of the same kind. The territory may belong to an individual or a family group, large or small. By establishing territories animals ensure that they have plenty of room in which to find food.

South American howler monkeys warn other groups of howler monkeys to keep away by making a lot of noise. Many other animals mark the boundaries of the territories with strong scents. Fights sometimes break out on territory boundaries, but intruders usually turn back as soon as the territory owner puts on a show of strength. A growl or the baring of teeth, or even the mere puffing up of the feathers, may be enough to frighten an intruder away.

A territory is not necessarily permanent. An animal or a group may defend an area of good food for just a few days or weeks, and then move on to establish a new one elsewhere.

HOME ON THE RANGE
Many other animals, including chimpanzees and gorillas, spend all of their lives roaming areas known as home ranges. These may cover hundreds of square kilometres or, in the case of small animals, be no bigger than a football pitch. Home ranges are not defended like territories. They often overlap those of other

▼ These male strawberry arrow-poison frogs are fighting for a territory. The wrestling match may continue for hours until the weaker frog gives up.

▶ The umbrella bird has a fleshy wattle hanging from its chest which it inflates to attract a mate.

DISPLAY GROUNDS

DURING the breeding season the males of some birds and mammals gather in small areas and compete with each other to put on the best displays to attract females. These communal display grounds are not true territories and they are called leks. Several rainforest butterflies also gather in leks. The males release scent signals and the females choose the males with the strongest signals. The scents often come from the nectar that the butterflies collect from flowers. This glasswing butterfly is one of many rainforest species that attract females with scents.

groups or families and neighbouring groups of animals may meet and feed together, especially in areas with plenty of food.

BREEDING TERRITORIES

Territories are especially important when animals are rearing families. This is generally the only time that animals settle down and make homes. Most birds, for example, build and occupy their nests only during the breeding season. The territory around the nest is defended by one or both parents, and its size depends on the amount of food available. Large territories are needed if food is scarce.

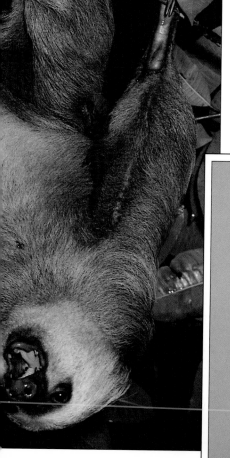

◀ Male sloths advertise their presence by smearing smelly secretions on to tree branches. Other males keep away, but females are attracted by the smell.

▼ The male three-wattled bellbird defends a large territory and attracts as many females to it as he can with his loud booming calls.

❊ Attracting a Mate ❊

PRODUCING A NEW generation is of vital importance for every species and for most animals this means finding a mate. Like humans, many rainforest animals use colour and scent, songs and dances, and other courtship behaviour to attract a mate. Female insects and mammals often attract males with a scent that tells them they are ready to mate. Male birds and bush-crickets lure their females with songs. Many birds also dance in front of the females and display their beautiful feathers.

Courtship songs and other displays bring males and females together and also get them into the right mood for mating. When animals mate, sperm passes from the males to the females and joins with the females' eggs. This is called fertilisation, and after it the eggs start to grow into new animals. Birds and many other animals lay their eggs soon after mating, but others, including most mammals, give birth to live young. The eggs develop inside, rather than outside, the females' bodies.

▲ During their courtship dance, the male scorpion drops a package of sperm and guides the female over it. She scoops it up and later gives birth to lots of babies.

▼ These giant millipedes from South America coil around each other to mate. The female will lay lots of eggs in the soil and abandon them.

▼ A male tree frog sings to attract a female. The balloon-like pouch under his neck vibrates and magnifies the sound. Each kind of frog has its own particular call so that it attracts only females of its own species.

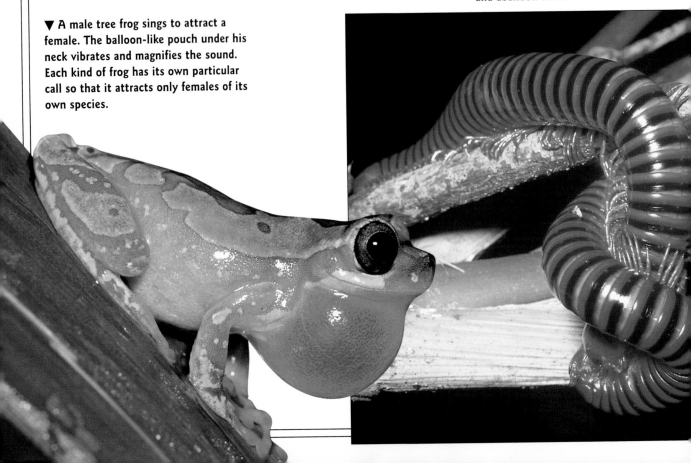

▲ A wire-tailed manakin and his helper jump up and down to attract a female. As soon as a female arrives, the younger bird is sent on his way.

▶ A male cock-of-the-rock will join his fellows in a communal courtship display. If he takes a female's fancy she will peck him on the rump to tell him.

WHAT A PERFORMANCE!

Male birds of paradise perform dazzling courtship displays that the females find irresistible. They swing acrobatically on the branches of trees or dance on the ground, twirling their long, colourful plumes in all directions. Each bird performs alone for one female and they soon become mates.

The male cock-of-the-rock has brilliant orange plumage, like a flame on the rainforest floor. Rather than each male courting a particular female, the males put on a communal display that is something between a dance and a gymnastic routine. The rather drab females watch as the males strut and then each one indicates her choice of partner by pecking him on the rump.

Manakin males employ one or more younger birds to assist with their display. The birds leap up and down on a branch as if bouncing on a trampoline. As one comes down, another goes up, singing all the while. When a female starts to show interest in the performance, the dominant bird whistles sharply and the assistants fly away, leaving the dominant bird to mate with the female.

COME INTO MY GARDEN

Bower birds are not particularly colourful, but they have a colourful courtship practice. To attract a mate, the male makes a love-nest. He builds a bower of twigs and then decorates it with flowers, berries, colourful shells, and even bits of coloured paper and glass. The females select the males with the best bowers. Some male bower birds seem to get jealous and steal the brightest objects from rival bowers. Sometimes they even destroy a rival bower. After mating in the bowers, the females go off to build their nests and rear their families alone.

LIGHTING THE FOREST

Fireflies, which are actually beetles, signal to their mates with flashes of light, just like torches going on and off. Each species has its own pattern of flashing, with a particular time interval between the flashes. So accurate is their sense of timing that they can recognise the flashes of their own species and ignore those of other species. Fireflies live in many parts of the world, but the most spectacular live in Southeast Asia. Thousands of males gather in certain mangrove trees and they all flash together like a neon sign. The females fly to the trees and mate with the males.

▲ A Wilson's bird of paradise entices the female with his beautiful plumage. Birds of paradise all live in New Guinea and neighbouring areas of Indonesia and on the northern tip of Australia.

ONE PARTNER OR MANY

IN THIS writhing ball of snakes (left) as many as ten male anacondas are attempting to mate with one female. In many species there is often intense competition for mates. One female may be courted by many males, and the males often fight each other. The female mates with the winner and, because he is strong, he will probably father healthy offspring. Most animals split up after mating and may never see each other again, although some males stay around long enough to help with the babies. A few animals stay together for life once they have mated, but most species have several or many partners during their lives.

Breeding All Year
. . . .

IN MOST parts of the world animals have definite breeding seasons. Birds, for example, usually breed in spring. Many tropical forests, especially those in the lowlands, remain warm and moist throughout the year, and plants never stop growing. Animals, like these delicate handkerchief butterflies performing their courtship dance, can breed at any time of the year. Many insects grow up in just three or four weeks and produce several generations in a year.

▼ Unable to resist the temptation, a female bower bird has accepted the male's invitation into his bower. After mating, the female will build a nest for her eggs and young.

⊛ INSECTS THAT LIVE TOGETHER ⊛

ANTS AND termites have the largest families of all rainforest creatures. They are social insects that live in huge family groups called colonies. The individuals all work for the good of the community as a whole.

ZILLION-MEMBER FAMILIES

Walk anywhere in the American rainforest at night and you are likely to see columns of ants marching along and waving bits of leaves above their heads and then disappearing underground. These are leaf-cutter ants. Their nests are often huge, as big as our living rooms. The ants dig out the soil themselves and pile it outside the nest. The heap of soil outside one nest in Brazil weighed 40 tonnes. A queen and up to eight million worker ants live in the nest, which may have over a thousand little rooms or chambers. The queen is the mother of all the ants in the nest. The workers are her daughters.

▲ Leaf-cutter ants can travel well over 100 metres to collect leaves, which they cut into neat sections. They often remove every leaf from a plant before attacking the next one.

PLANT PARTNERS

A NTS do not only work with each other, some enter into partnerships with the plants they live on. Many tropical plants, including the climbing palms or rattans and some of the acacia trees, give homes to fierce ants. The ants swarm out and sting any animal that starts to nibble the leaves. The plants are thus protected by their guests. Some of the plants actually provide food for the ants in the form of honey-like nectar. This carnivorous ant (right) is protecting a passion flower.

Many epiphytic plants have swollen bases that are riddled with small chambers in which various ants take up residence. The ants protect the plants from attack and their droppings also provide the plants with valuable food.

▼ Leaf-cutter ants are also called parasol ants because they hold the cut leaves like sunshades. Their nests (left) may be two metres or more deep and occupy many cubic metres.

FAMILY FARMS

To feed so many individuals leaf-cutter ants have evolved a remarkable skill. They have become farmers, growing tiny mushrooms in special gardens. Every day at sunset many thousands of the ants stream from their nests and head for the trees. They use their scissor-like jaws to carve pieces from the leaves, and then carry the pieces back to their nests. They give the leaf fragments to smaller workers. These smaller ants chew the leaf fragments into a soggy pulp, which they put into one of many special garden chambers. They add some of the fungus from an existing garden and often add their own droppings as a sort of manure. The fungus grows rapidly on the pulped leaves and soon covers them with fluffy threads. Little swellings form at the tips of the threads and the workers gather them for food. Old fungus gardens are regularly thrown on to the heap of soil around the nest.

TEEMING TERMITES

There are hundreds of different kinds of termites. They are like ants, but not related to them. Termites are all vegetarians, feeding on seeds, leaves and dead wood. Some of them cultivate fungi on dead leaves just like leaf-cutter ants. Termites do immense damage to buildings in rainforest areas and in other parts of the tropics.

Many termite species live under the ground or hidden in dead wood. Some make small nests on the branches of rainforest trees, others build huge mounds of earth. Some of them stick soil particles together with saliva to make roads from their nests to their feeding grounds. And some even build roofs over their roads so that they can reach their feeding grounds without exposing themselves to light or to their many enemies. Their pale, soft bodies are very nutritious and many birds and other animals like to eat them.

KING AND QUEEN

A large termite colony contains millions of insects and is ruled by a single queen who does nothing but lay eggs. Her sausage-like body pumps out as many as 30,000 eggs every day. The

▲ A termite nest has been damaged. Soldiers swarm over the exposed surface to attack the enemy, while the other termites scurry away to safety.

▼ This termite soldier specialises in chemical warfare. A group of such soldiers can quickly immobilise an attacker by firing streams of sticky fluid from their tubular snouts.

AIR-CONDITIONED HOMES

BIG termite nests contain hundreds of rooms in which the insects store their food and rear the youngsters, and the rooms are linked by hundreds of narrow passages. Some of the biggest nests even have air-conditioning systems to stop them from getting too hot. Each kind of termite has developed its own system. In one scheme, chimney-like tubes allow the hot, stale air to escape. Fresh air flows in through holes near the bottom and keeps the whole nest fresh and cool.

Termites living in rainforests often build mushroom-shaped nests or else they add umbrella-shaped roofs (right) to keep the rain out.

other termites work hard to feed her and keep her clean. The queen lives with a king, who is much smaller than she is. The other termites in the colony are all the children of the king and queen. Most of them are workers and, although they are blind, they collect all the food and do all the building work. There are also some soldier termites, with big heads and jaws, whose job is to defend the colony. They bite anything that tries to break into the nest, although anteaters and some other animals do not seem to mind their bites.

The termites in a colony are always licking each other and exchanging food. This helps to spread pheromones, the chemical messengers that ensure that they all behave properly and do the right things at the right times. Many of the pheromones come from the queen.

From time to time, the termite colony rears new kings and queens, and these fly out from the nest in huge swarms. The birds and other animals have a real feast for a few hours. The few termites that avoid the predators and get back to earth break off their wings and pair up to start new colonies.

❋ FROG FAMILIES ❋

FROGS cannot live far from water because they have thin skins. They quickly shrivel and die in dry air. They also have to lay their eggs in water. In most places they live near ponds, but in the rainforests it is so damp that they can make their homes in the trees. The forests are also full of insects so the frogs are never short of food.

Hundreds of different species of frogs live in rainforests. Many spend all their lives in the trees and do not even come down to breed. They are active mainly in the evening and at night, when there are fewer predators around to eat them. To attract females the males sing loudly and the night air is full of their assorted clicks, squeaks and whistles, some of which are surprisingly musical. When in full song, the forest frogs drown out nearly all the other sounds.

▶ Mosquito larvae living in rainwater pools provide food for baby frogs.

▲ A male glass frog, transparent and almost invisible on a leaf, sits close to its jelly-like masses of eggs to protect them. It will also bring water from time to time to prevent the eggs from drying up.

◄ Leaping for love! This flying frog glides down from the tree-tops to mate and lay its eggs on leaves overhanging water. The tadpoles fall into the water when they hatch.

► The colourful underside of this barred leaf frog helps it attract a mate and break up its outline as it moves. Tree frogs do not normally hop like most other frogs, they crawl slowly on their long slender legs.

Tree-Top Nurseries

The branches of the rainforest trees are covered with various small plants called epiphytes. Many of these plants collect rainwater in their crowns of spiky leaves and some tree frogs lay their eggs in the little pools. Mosquito larvae and lots of other small creatures also live in the pools and provide food for the tadpoles that hatch from the eggs. Hidden among the spiky leaves, the tadpoles are also protected from many of their enemies.

WRESTLING MALES

Strawberry arrow-poison frogs are as brightly coloured and poisonous as their name suggests, though the poison is not used aggressively. Males adopt territories on the ground, each one choosing an area with plenty of water-holding plants, such as bromeliads, that will provide homes for the tadpoles. The male guards his territory vigorously and is unceasing in his efforts to attract females, calling to them continuously. Any other male that enters the area is seen off. Neighbouring males often fight, clutching each other like wrestlers and rolling over and over on the forest floor. They shove and kick each other, often until both are exhausted (see page 6).

REMARKABLE MOTHER

Once a female strawberry arrow-poison frog has accepted the male's advances and mated, she lays her eggs under a dead leaf. She lays no more than about ten eggs, because they are going to be well cared for. The male sits by them for a couple of weeks and then the tadpoles emerge and crawl on to the female's back. She carries them to the bromeliad plants and drops them into the little pools. There is plenty of water for them to swim in, but not a great deal of food, so she usually drops just one tadpole into each plant. Later, she tops up the food supply by laying extra eggs in the plants. The tadpoles use these eggs for food.

POND BUILDERS

One Brazilian tree frog builds its own private pool in shallow water at the edge of a pond or stream. The male collects mud with his front

FROG IN A POUCH

MARSUPIAL frogs are good at looking after their families. The female of this pygmy marsupial frog from Venezuela (above) has a large pouch on her back and, after fertilising the eggs, the male guides them into the pouch.

▼ One by one, a mother strawberry arrow-poison frog carries her tadpoles on her back to its own private pool in a bromeliad.

▲ Safe in its nursery pool, a baby arrow-poison frog waits for its mother. She will check that there is enough water in the pool and lay more eggs for it to eat.

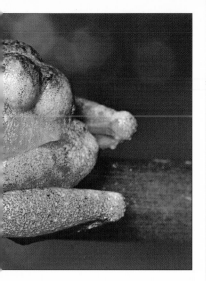

The eggs hatch in the pouch and the tadpoles live there for a while, nourished by food stored in the eggs. Even when they turn into froglets, the young of some species continue to be carried by their parents. They are not released into the water until they are quite large.

NESTS OF BUBBLES

SEVERAL kinds of frogs, including these Central American tungara frogs, protect their eggs by covering them with foam. The female produces a lot of slime with her eggs, and then the male and female whip it into a foam with their feet. The outer layer of foam may dry and form a hard skin, keeping the inner layers moist, but the females of some species keep the whole nest moist by periodically collecting water and spraying it over the foam. These foam nests are usually formed on leaves overhanging a pool or stream, and when the eggs hatch the foam turns to liquid and the tadpoles fall into the water below.

▼ A Darwin's frog male with two of his offspring. Until they are big enough to fend for themselves, the adult frog keeps them in his throat pouch.

feet and, using the broad pads on the tips of his fingers, moulds it into a circular wall about 30 cm across. When complete, the wall stands about 10 cm above the surrounding water. The frog then starts his love song with a loud, rather monotonous metallic call that sounds like a hammer on steel. This none the less attracts the female, who lays her eggs in the pool, where they are safe from most enemies. The tadpoles stay inside the wall for a while, but eventually it crumbles and they escape into the surrounding water.

❂ FORESTS FULL OF NESTS ❂

THERE IS ample nest-building material in the rainforests and a spectacular variety of nests. Birds are particularly ingenious. Their nest-building skills include sewing, weaving and sticking plant materials together to make cosy nurseries for their eggs and nestlings.

WEAVER ANTS

Though they are highly skilled, weaver ants are not well named. Rather than weaving, they make their nests by sticking leaves together in a remarkable way. The ants pull several leaves together to form a bag or

▼ Green weaver ants live in the tropical forests of Africa, Asia and Australia. Each colony defends its territory against ants from other nests.

▶ This leaf-rolling spider from Borneo guards its eggs and young inside a rolled leaf. The female also shelters there while waiting for prey to arrive.

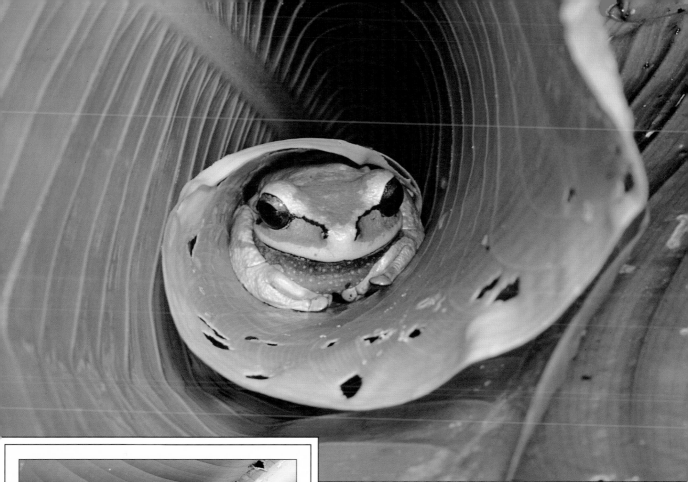

TREE-TOP TENTS

SEVERAL kinds of bats make neat little shelters for themselves by nibbling through the veins of leaves so that the leaf blades flop down like tent roofs. The tents keep the bats perfectly dry, despite the forest's heavy rainfall, and also conceal them from predators. Some of the bats even have their babies in the tents and leave them there while they go out to feed.

▲ Masked puddle frogs make temporary homes in the curled young leaves of heliconia plants, where they stay moist and hidden from their enemies during the daytime.

pouch by gripping the edges with their hind feet and their powerful jaws. If the gap is too wide for one ant to stretch across it, two or more link their legs to form chains, and then they all pull together to bring the edges of the leaves into line.

Then comes the really fascinating bit: ants carrying young grubs start to run in a zigzag fashion along the joins. The grubs give out strands of sticky silk, which the adults fix to each side of the join. The silk soon hardens and the leaves are held firmly together. A mature nest may be nearly as big as a football but, because the leaves are still attached to the tree and remain green, the nests are not easy to see. And any animal that does find a nest is in for a shock, because the weaver ants are bad-tempered and bite viciously.

WEAVING BIRDS

The male oropendola courts the female with a noisy dance, during which he raises his tail and wings and bows so low that he almost topples from his perch. The birds nest in colonies and often build dozens of nests in a single tree. The nests are built by the females, while their mates keep watch and sing from nearby perches. Each nest is rather like a large sock, up to a metre long and skilfully woven from strips of palm leaves. Each one hangs from the swaying tip of a branch, where few enemies can reach it. Several kinds of oropendolas live in the American rainforests, each one building to a slightly different design.

The weaver birds of Africa build similar nests, but there it is the male who starts the building work. When he is about half way through he tries to interest a female in his

▼ Part of a colony of chestnut-headed oropendolas in Central America. Strong winds can damage the nests, so the birds usually build them in fairly sheltered spots.

TREE-TOP CRADLES

HUMMINGBIRDS include the smallest of all birds. Twigs and most other plant materials are too big and coarse to make good nesting material for these delicate creatures. Instead they gather plant hairs and silk from spiders' webs to build little cup-shaped nests. Some include soft petals as well to make a satiny lining for their nestlings' cradle.

◀ The straight-billed hermit, a kind of hummingbird, builds its nest with plant hairs and spider silk and fixes it in a rather precarious-looking position at the tip of a large, drooping leaf.

▲ These two blue-throated goldentail hummingbird chicks are about to leave the flimsy, hammock-like nest, made largely from spider silk, that has been their home for about three weeks.

▼ The nest of the white-throated spadebill, made from tightly-woven plant fibres, is fixed to a slender twig.

work, and if she likes what she sees, she moves in and finishes the job. Most weaver birds live in open country, but the village weaver likes to build on the edges of forest villages. Its ball-shaped nests hang from the tips of branches and palm leaves, and weigh them down like large fruits.

A TAILORED NEST

The tailor bird deserves its name, because it really does sew its nest together. It chooses a large leaf or sometimes two smaller ones and sews the edges together to form a bag. Its slender, sharply pointed beak makes an excellent needle. The thread is made from cottony fibres stripped from plants and spun into longer strands, or from bark fibres or even silk strands from spiders' webs. As the tailor bird sews, it ties knots in the thread to keep it in place. When the sewing is complete, the bird lines the nest with soft fibres. Because the tailor bird's nest is made from living leaves still attached to the tree, it is hard to distinguish amongst the forest vegetation. Tailor birds live in southern Asia, in and around the forests and in many other habitats. When living close to villages, they often sew their nests with bits of string and cotton discarded by the villagers.

WALLED UP

Hornbills have huge beaks that they use for stretching out to reach fruit at the tips of slender branches. Their bills are long but very light and not at all powerful. They are certainly no use for excavating a nest hole. So, when the female is ready to nest, she has to find an existing hole in a tree that suits her needs. She settles inside and for up to three months afterwards remains a prisoner in the hole. Her mate brings her mud and she uses it like cement to block up the entrance hole until only a narrow slit remains – just big enough for her to poke her beak out to take food from the male. Inside her prison, she lays her eggs and rears her nestlings. When the chicks are two or three weeks old, the mother bird breaks out of her prison, but the young birds immediately seal up the hole again to keep themselves safe from predators. The male and female both continue to bring food for the growing nestlings. Only when they are strong enough to fly do the little birds come out of prison.

▲ A male knobbed hornbill from Indonesi perches by its nest hole, which the female has started to wall up with mud.

◄ A male resplendent quetzal feeds its hungry chick with its favourite food – a nutritious wild avocado.

▲ The six-sided paper cells containing the grubs are clearly visible on the underside of this wasp nest.

◄ The slaty-backed nightingale-thrush from Central America builds a bulky nest with mosses and other plants and fixes it firmly in a bush.

PAPER NESTS

Many species of wasps live in the rainforests and some build remarkable nests of paper – the chewed fibres of plants. The nest is started by the queen after she has mated. She chews up the paper and spreads it out in layers that she forms into little cells where she lays her eggs. The eggs hatch and eventually turn into small female worker wasps. They set to work immediately, building new cells for new eggs. The eggs turn into larvae and the workers feed them with food they have collected. This is usually the flesh of insects and other small animals that the wasps have caught and torn to pieces with their tough jaws. They chew the flesh and swallow it, and bring it up again to feed the grubs in the nest. These grubs grow into more workers, which build more cells for more eggs: the nest grows and grows.

◄ This male golden-browed chlorophonia from Central America has collected material for its cup-shaped nest that will hold up to five nestlings. It belongs to a group of brightly-coloured birds called tanagers.

❖ MONKEYS AND APES ❖

MOST RAINFOREST mammals are solitary creatures that rear their young alone, with or without males in attendance. Monkeys and apes often form large family clans that fiercely guard a territory. But not all monkeys form clans. Some live in small family groups, with just a male and female and their youngsters. Others form harems, in which one male lives with several females and their youngsters.

Monkeys and apes do not make real homes, even when rearing their babies. They wander freely over their territories or home ranges and sleep wherever they happen to be when it gets dark.

▶ The vivid colours on the male mandrill's face warn intruders to keep away and younger members of the group to keep their place. They also attract females to mate with him.

TROOPS OF MONKEYS

Howler monkeys live in clans, or troops, each containing several adult males and females and youngsters of all ages. There may be 30 or more monkeys in a clan and they 'talk' to each other with a wide variety of sounds. Clicking sounds help to keep the clan together when scampering through the tree-tops. Loud howls warn of approaching danger, but the loudest sounds are reserved for territorial defence. When they wake in the morning, the animals set up a deafening chorus of howls and roars that can be heard as much as 5 km away. This frightening outburst warns other clans of howler monkeys to keep away for the rest of the day.

◀ A crab-eating macaque from Bali sits on the remains of an ancient temple and tends its baby. Babies are much appreciated by all the monkeys in a troop. They are often passed round for other females to cuddle them.

▼ A crested black macaque keeps watch for any dangers that threaten as it sits on the ground with its baby.

◀ Not all monkeys form large clans. Some, like these golden-lion tamarins, live in small family groups of just a male and female with their youngsters.

CHIMPANZEE CLANS

Chimpanzees are apes and the nearest living relatives of human beings. They live in Africa in loosely organised clans that can contain 100 or more individuals, although small groups often break away and wander off on their own for a while. A clan has no obvious leader and, although the adult males sometimes boss the others about, all the clan members usually get on well with each other.

Chimpanzees are equally at home on the ground and in the trees. They usually sleep high in the trees, where they are safe from leopards. They make new, springy beds nearly every night by twisting leafy branches together. Even when they have young babies, chimpanzees do not make real nests.

Baby chimpanzees are carried around by their mothers as soon as they are born. There are always babies in the clan and the females all help to look after them. The young chimpanzees stay close to their mothers for five or six years, and spend a lot of this time playing with other youngsters. The males take little interest in their babies.

▶ A silverback gorilla is respected and obeyed by the whole troop. Occasionally he may be challenged by younger males hoping to win his females, and in time will be too old and tired to defend his harem.

▼ A young chimpanzee begs an older member of the clan for a share of its meat. Watching how the adults collect fruit and catch and kill food is an important part of a youngster's training.

▲ Orang-utans are large apes of Southeast Asia. Adults live alone, although babies stay with their mothers for at least three years.

GROOMING

ONKEYS and apes spend many hours contentedly grooming each other. One animal combs and searches the fur of another. They lick and run their fingers through each other's fur, and both partners seem to gain pleasure from the activity. When an animal wants to be groomed, it usually approaches another and offers an arm or some other part of its body. As well as removing lice and other parasites and keeping the fur clean, grooming is socially beneficial. It helps to calm the animals and keep all the members of the clan on good terms. Animals that have spent time grooming each other are likely to help each other in times of trouble.

GORILLAS

The gorilla is the largest of the apes. A big male, standing nearly two metres high and weighing nearly 200 kg, can look very fierce, but the animals are really very peaceful. Gorillas live in the forests of West and Central Africa. They are too heavy to do much climbing, so they live mainly on the ground. At night they sleep on beds or cushions made from leafy branches. These are usually just above the ground, although small gorillas may make their beds in the trees.

Gorillas live in small clans. There are usually between 10 and 15 animals in a clan, and it is ruled by an old male. He has silvery grey hair on his back and is called a silverback. The clan also contains several females and youngsters of various ages, and there may be one or more blackback males. These are fully grown gorillas, but without the silvery grey hair. Every animal knows its place in the clan and there is hardly ever any fighting. Junior members always move aside for older ones.

The silverback makes all the decisions, such as when to get up in the morning, which way to go, and when to eat. Young gorillas stay with their mothers for about six years, during which time they learn the meaning of all the sounds and signs used by the clan members. They soon learn who is the boss of the clan.

▼ A curious young gorilla sets off to explore. Gorillas have few enemies. The biggest threat to their survival is from the destruction of their forest habitat by humans.

❈ GLOSSARY ❈

Arrow-poison frog Any of a number of South American frogs whose poison is used on darts and arrows. Also called poison-dart frogs.

Breed To breed is to reproduce, or have babies.

Bromeliad Any of a number of plants, related to pineapples, with crowns of stiff leaves. The crowns hold pools of water. Many bromeliads grow as epiphytes on the branches of trees.

Camouflage Skin colours and patterns that help an animal blend with its surroundings and avoid the attention of predators.

Canopy The 'roof' of the rainforest, formed by the leafy branches of the trees. It is usually about 30 metres above the ground and it cuts off most of the light from the forest floor.

Clan The name given to a group of monkeys or apes that live together like a big family.

Communal Living together as part of an organised community.

Courtship The behaviour of males and females that brings them together for mating and reproduction.

Dominant The dominant animal in a community is the leader – the individual that controls the others.

Epiphyte Any plant that grows on another, especially on the branches of a tree, but takes no food from it. Ferns, orchids and bromeliads are common epiphytes in the rainforests.

Equator An imaginary line around the centre of the earth, midway between the north and south poles.

Fertilisation The joining of a sperm from a male animal with an egg from a female.

Fungi (singular fungus) Plant-like organisms that grow without sunlight and take their food from living or dead plants and animals. They reproduce by scattering minute dust-like particles called spores. Mushrooms and moulds are all fungi.

Habitat The natural home of a plant or animal species. It may be a whole forest or just a tree trunk, or even a pool of water trapped by a plant.

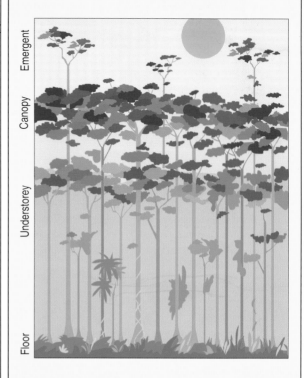

▲ A rainforest has layers of vegetation. Low shrubs grow on the forest floor, and slender young trees form an understorey below the vast, dense canopy of tree-tops. At intervals taller trees called emergents poke their heads through the canopy. All the plants are trying to get a share of the sunlight.

Harem A group of adult females living with, and controlled by, a single male. The male mates with all the females in the group.

Home range An area inhabited by an animal or a group of animals but not defended against other animals of the same kind.

Larva (plural larvae) Stage in the development of some animals. Caterpillars and tadpoles are larvae.

Mangrove An evergreen tree whose stilt-like roots form dense tangles in coastal swamps.

Mate Animals mate with each other to produce offspring. The male passes sperm from his body to combine with the eggs of the female. Each is the other's mate.

Metamorphosis The changes in shape of some animals that take place as they grow up.

Nestling A young bird that has not yet left its nest.

Pheromone A chemical signal or scent given out by one animal and causing another animal of the same kind to behave in a particular way. Pheromones help to keep ant colonies working

ENDANGERED!

R AINFORESTS are vitally important to the well-being of the world but they are in danger of destruction. Many of the animals and plants featured in this book are under threat from forest clearance. If you are interested in knowing more about rainforests and in helping to conserve them, you may find these addresses and websites useful.

Friends of the Earth, Rainforest Campaign, *26-28 Underwood Street, London N1 7JQ*

Rainforest Foundation, *A5 City Cloisters, 188-96 Old St, London EC1V 9FR*

Worldwide Fund for Nature
WWF (Australia), *Level 5, 725 George Street, Sydney, NSW 2000*
WWF (South Africa), *116 Dorp Street, Stellenbosch 7600*
WWF (UK), *Panda House, Weyside Park, Cattershall Lane, Godalming, Surrey GU17 1XR*

Worldwide Fund for Nature
http://www.wwf-uk.org

Friends of the Earth
http://www.foe.co.uk

Environmental Education Network
http://envirolink.org.enviroed/

Rainforest Foundation
http://rainforestfoundationuk.org

Rainforest Preservation Foundation
http://www.flash.net/~rpf/

Survival International
http://www.survival.org.uk

Sustainable Development
http://iisd1.iisd.ca/

Rainforest Action Network
http://www.igc.apc.org/ran/intro.html

◀ **The map shows the location of the world's main rainforest areas.**

properly, and they also bring male and female animals together for mating.

gorilla, because of the silvery-grey hair on his back.

Plumage The feathers of a bird.

Plume The name given to any particularly large or attractive feather.

Predator Any animal that hunts and kills other animals for food.

Primate Any member of the order of mammals containing the monkeys and apes. Human beings are primates, and so are tarsiers and bushbabies.

Pupa The stage in an insect's life during which it changes from a larva or caterpillar into an adult.

Saliva A fluid secreted by glands in or around the mouth. It lubricates food and often helps to digest it. Many insects mix saliva with mud and other materials and use the mixture for building their nests.

Silverback The name given to a mature male

Social insects Insects that live in communities and work together for the good of the whole group. They include termites and ants and some bees and wasps. Each community is headed by one or more queens and all the other insects are the children of these queens.

Sperm A male cell that can join with a female egg cell to produce a new cell from which a new animal can grow.

Tadpole Name given to the young stages of frogs and toads.

Territory An area inhabited by an animal or a group of animals, and defended against other animals of the same kind.

Tropical Describes the tropics – the warm areas around the equator.

Vegetarian Any animal that feeds mainly on plants.